MONEY BOOT CAMP

Financial Literacy for Teens

by Chella Diaz

Courtesy of:

Published by:

PYP Publishing Group

Address: 725 Fawn Court

City, State Zip: Vacaville, CA 95687

For Further information please visit www.PYPPublishingGroup.com or call: 415-599-4475

Money Boot Camp; Financial Literacy for Teens

©2013 Chella Diaz

Cover Design and Editor: Jaqueline Kyle

PYP Publishing Group

www.PYPPublishingGroup.com

First Printing: 2013

ISBN: 0991041607

CONTENTS

INTRODUCTION

I rarely read book introductions because authors often talk about themselves and I don't care about their dog or meaningless dedications.

This book was written to give you the information about money that I didn't learn until later in my life. My parents never talked to me about money and schools didn't help me understand the realities of money. I have spent a lot of time trying to understand money.

Understand money? Sounds dumb, right? You have money and you spend it or save it. But there's a lot more you need to know in order to become wealthy so you can enjoy life.

The information in this book is what I have passed on to my teenagers and taught to many students. I want you to be better off than me. I could have been very wealthy if I were money smart when I was your age.

Anyway, I truly dedicate this book to you. You are the reason I am writing this book, as nothing will bring me more joy than to help you plan your journey to wealth and happiness.

Chella

ONE

1.0 TALKING ABOUT MONEY IS BORING

Let's be honest here, most people would rather wash dishes than talk about money, which can be a boring subject. I don't want to bore you talking about finance, so I will cut to the chase with the basics and give you food for thought to help you understand how you can become wealthy.

I want you to stop reading for a minute and imagine how your life will change when you are wealthy. Think of the house you will be living in, the car you will be driving, and the vacations you will take. Is being rich and having a lot of money boring to you now? Having a lot of money enables you to do things for yourself and others. Have you ever heard the saying, "Money isn't everything?" Take it from me that only rich people say that, as for many poor people, "Money IS everything."

The knowledge you learn in this workbook will not be boring if you keep in mind that you will become rich. If you don't learn from it, it may affect your life. Don't laugh or you may end up struggling for money like most people, who don't have money knowledge. Creating wealth is a journey following the money map of knowledge. Your journey begins right now.

1.1 SPENDING PLANS AND SPENDING SMART

Many people will tell you that you need to have a savings plan. It's a plan where you save a certain amount of money every week or month. We often run out of money by the end of the week, so this often doesn't work when you're starting out.

Others will tell you to create a budget. It's simple to create a budget when you know how much money comes in during a week or month and then plan on how you are going to spend it. Those last two words, "spend it," are why I'm not a big fan of budgets.

A budget has buckets or categories of how much you plan to spend for things within a specific amount of time, usually a month.

As an example you may have a lunch budget of $100 a month and a movie budget of $50 a month. The problem with budgets is that most people will spend every dollar in the budget. If you knew you could spend $50 a month for movies, you probably would spend $50 on movies every month. If I told someone they could spend $200 every month at the mall because it's in their monthly budget, they probably would spend $200 every month. Remember this: *People will spend every dollar in their budget for things they both need and want.*

I find it much easier to come up with a simple spending plan instead of a savings plan or a budget. An easy way to keep track of your spending is by writing down all of the things you spend money on such as movies, chips, gum, clothes, going out to eat, or anything else you purchase.

Here's my spending plan for the last week. Everyday, I simply wrote down how I spent my money.

My Spending Plan for a Week

Saturday	$10 movies, $10 popcorn and drink, $10 for dinner at Pizza Hut
Sunday	$25 for shoes at Mall, $4 soda, $25 for a hat
Monday	$30 for gas, $20 for groceries
Tuesday	$15 lunch at Olive Garden
Wednesday	Nothing
Thursday	$5 breakfast at McDonald's (fruit), $4 Starbucks, $7 dinner at the Mall
Friday	$5 Veggie sandwich at Subway for lunch, $4 Starbucks

It may not look like much, but it adds up to $174 during the week. Let's look at it from a spending plan's view of <u>Need</u> or <u>Want</u>. You can't live easily without the things you *need*, but you have a choice with the things you *want*.

Need	Want
$30 gas	$10 movies
$20 groceries	$10 popcorn and drinks
$25 shoes	$10 dinner at Pizza Hut
	$4 soda
	$25 hat
	$15 lunch at Olive Garden
	$5 breakfast at McDonald's
	$4 Starbucks
	$7 dinner at mall
	$5 Subway for lunch
	$4 Starbucks

So, I spent $99 on things I want and spent $75 on things I need. I didn't have a choice on the things I needed, but I did on the things I wanted. It doesn't seem like a big deal to spend $14 a day on things I want, but over a year (52 weeks) this adds up to almost $5,200! Now, that's a big deal! Remember this amount of $5,200. We'll use this number to start you towards becoming a millionaire.

Okay, so create your spending plan for the next week by tracking everything you buy. Do it by the end of every day for a week. Multiply it by 52 weeks to figure how much you spend in a year. The following week you can make it a game to see how much you can control your *wants*. As we talk more about money, you'll understand why this lesson will be worth its weight in gold.

Keeping track of how you spend your money enables you to see how you can save money. Because I wrote down my spending plan I was able to see what I *need* instead of *want*. I could have saved $99 by only buying things I needed.

1.2 SPENDING SMART EVERYDAY

Spending smart means that you spend less than what the price tag says. Stores love it when you purchase things at full price because they make more money. Would you rather help the store or yourself?

- Watch for sales and specials offers.

- Resist impulse buying.

- Limit the cash you carry.

- Avoid ATM fees. (ATM fees are charged when you use your debit card at another bank instead of your bank. For example, you have your account with Chase and you withdraw money at Wells Fargo.)

Save money by eating at home or bringing your lunch to school and work. Make a shopping list for the grocery store and only buy what is on your list. Look at your list to make sure you have all the things that you *need* and remove things that you *want*.

1.3 SPENDING SMART ON YOUR WISH LIST

We all need to buy things that cost a lot of money like a computer, car, or a college education. When you spend a lot of money on your wish list you need to take your time and think about your decision.

First, ask yourself if it is something you *need* or *want*. Think about your wish list often, as it will help you to cut back spending on things that you want, but don't need.

Decide how much you can spend on your wish list items and still pay for the things that you need.

It does not matter how much money you make...what matters is how much money you spend.

Visit www.moneybasics101.com for tips that show you how to get things you want by making different choices.

Two

2.0 How To Win The Lotto Without Playing

Many people try to become millionaires by playing the Lottery and picking the winning six numbers. The odds of winning Super Lotto are over 1 in 41,000,000.

Let's compare your odds of winning the Lotto to better understand your chances. You are 4 times more likely to become president, 71 times more likely to be struck by lightning, and 1,800 times more likely to be a professional athlete than to win the Lotto.

The easier way to become a millionaire without playing the Lotto is by being smart with your money. You don't have to save a million dollars to become a millionaire, but you do need to use the time value of money. It may sound complicated, but it's simply about the words, "time" and "money."

Remember in the first chapter, where you saved over $5,000 a year on *wants* instead of *needs*? We will now put the money you saved in one year into our money time machine.

2.1 Rule of 72

If you lend me $100 and at the end of the year I pay you $110 back, then you earned $10. Another way of saying this is that you earned 10% interest ($10/$100=10%) or had an annual rate of return (return on your investment) of 10%.

There is a way to estimate how much time it takes to double your money at different rates of interest. This is called the Rule of 72. How it works is that you take 72 and divide it by the interest your money is earning. The result is how long it will take to double your money.

For example, if you were earning 10% interest, you would divided 72 by 10 to learn that it will take 7.2 years to double your money.

The Rule of 72 is "Money will double every 7.2 years at 10%." By remembering this rule, you can apply it many ways. Using the Rule of 72, let's figure how long it takes to double your money at 15%.

Using the Rule of 72:

If Money doubles every 7.2 years at 10%, then we could say

Money doubles every 4.8 years at 15%,

You get the picture.

Note: The Rule of 72 is an estimate, but it is a quick way to make an educated guess of the value of money over time.

In the example below you can see for yourself that the Rule of 72 not only works in this case, but that it's much easier to remember than having to do the math. How long will $5,000 take to double in value at 10%?

Year	Value	Interest
0	$5,000	$0
1	$5,500	$500 (10% times $5,000)
2	$6,050	$550 (10% times $5,500)
3	$6,655	$605 (10% times $6,050)
4	$7,320	$665 (10% times $6,665)
5	$8,052	$732 (10% times $7,320)
6	$8,857	$805 (10% times $8,052)
7	$9,743	$885 (10% times $8,857)
7 +2 mos	$10,000	$257 (10% for 2 months)

Notice that the interest amount for each year gets bigger as the years increase. The interest starts at $500 and almost doubles to $974. That is because the interest gets added to the value every year. It's like getting interest on your interest. This is called compound interest. We'll talk more about compound interest in a bit, as it's very important for you to understand the value of this.

Let's have fun with the Rule of 72 to see how our millionaire journey plays out. In the first chapter, we started by controlling our *wants* versus *needs* for about $14 a day. In one year we saved $5,000. Let's look at what will happen to that money if we earn an average of 10% per year.

Year	Value	Interest
0	$5,000	$0
7.2	$10,000	10% per year
14.4	$20,000	10% per year
21.6	$40,000	10% per year
28.8	$80,000	10% per year
36.0	$160,000	10% per year
43.2	$320,000	10% per year
50.4	$640,000	10% per year

After 50 years it was worth about $640,000. Guess how much it will be worth if you wait another 7.2 years?

2.2 COMPOUND INTEREST KICKS BIG (YOU'LL SEE)

I told you talking about money could be boring. Hopefully, you have more interest now after learning about how quickly your money can grow and make you rich.

The annual rate of return on your money is huge in determining how much money you will end up with. I'd like to introduce you to your new friend, <u>compound interest</u>! It's when the interest amount just keeps getting bigger and bigger. We know that the Rule of 72 tells us that your money will double faster at a higher rate, but you will be amazed at how the rate of interest affects your money.

Let's take our $5,000 and I'll show you how it adds up at different rates using the power of compound interest.

Years	0.20%	10.00%	15.00%
5	$5,050	$7,986	$10,054
10	$5,101	$12,862	$20,108
20	$5,204	$33,360	$80,432
30	$5,309	$86,526	$321,728
40	$5,416	$224,426	$1,286,912
50	$5,525	$582,103*	$5,147,648

*variation from previous table is the difference between estimating with Rule of 72 and calculating the equation

Every column started with just $5,000. Look how the bottom numbers grew! Notice what a 5% difference makes to the bottom row between 10% and 15%. It's much more than just a 5% difference!

2.3 RICH PEOPLE ARE SMART ABOUT MONEY

You now have learned that by being smart with your money, you too can be rich. There are thousands of millionaires who are regular people that have regular jobs such as teachers, mechanics, and nurses. Even your neighbor could be a millionaire! All millionaires have one thing in common. They are smart about money.

Last note. If you look at those compound interest numbers in Section 2.2, you'll see the first column grew to only $5,525 after 50 years at the rate of .20%. That's the highest rate that one of the largest banks is paying to their savings account customers. Take a look at the signs on the tallest buildings in any major city and you'll see many bank names. Guess who paid for those buildings? It's the people who aren't smart about money. Guess who made $525 after fifty years and who made $500,000 with their money?

Three

3.0 Borrow like the rich or spend like the poor

I used to wonder why rich people borrowed money. It made no sense to me why they wouldn't just pay for their house in cash instead of getting a loan. Both rich and poor people spend money. It's how you spend your money that makes you rich or poor in the end. Don't forget about the lesson of *wants* versus *needs*.

While reviewing two loan applications:

1. Doctor's loan application, he made $250,000 a year. He had no savings, no investments, and spent all of his money every month. He spent like the poor because he spent everything he made. The bank would not lend him any money because he was broke, even though he was paid very well. You don't have to be poor to spend like the poor.

2. Auto Mechanic shop owner, he made $100,000 a year. He had $25,000 in savings and $50,000 in investments. He spent his money on needs and saved the rest of his money. The bank approved his loan. In the bank's point of view, Mr. Mechanic knew how to manage his money.

3.1 Why Borrow Money and not pay cash?

Many wealthy people understand why borrowing money is better than using their own cash. Let me share why this makes sense so you'll be money smart.

Let's say that you have followed the lessons in this book and over time you had $1,000,000 that you wanted to invest in a business. The business generates $200,000 in income per year after all expenses.

Since you are money smart, your $1,000,000 has been in the stock market earning 15% or $150,000 per year. Okay, we'll use some or all of the stock to buy our business. We will do it two different ways. Borrow money like the rich or spend it like the poor.

Buying your first business. Let's see if it makes sense to pay cash or borrow money.

<u>Let's pay cash</u>

Congratulations! You are a business owner.

1. Sell the stock for a $1,000,000

2. Buy the business for $1,000,000

3. Your business is generating $200,000 net income per year

Let's borrow money

Congratulations! You are a business owner.

1. You sell $250,000 of your stock as a down payment, so you're still left with $750,000 of stock. At 15% it will generate $112,500 per year.

2. You borrow $750,000 at an interest rate of 7%, which has an interest cost of $52,500 per year.

3. Buy the business for $1,000,000

4. Your business is generating $200,000 net income per year.

5. Total income is $112,500 from stock+ $200,000 from business = $312,500

6. Net income is $312,500 - $52,500 (cost of loan) = $260,000 per year

By borrowing money to buy your business you have made $60,000 more every year than if you paid cash for it. That's $600,000 in ten years! Imagine using the Rule of 72 and it could be $1,200,000! It's amazing how borrowing money can make you more money.

FOUR

4.0 BENEFITS OF A BUDGET

Now that you know how you spend your money, let's take it one step further.

You probably already understand the value of a budget. Let's say you have a budget of $4 for lunch. The food costs $3 and the drink costs $1. You know you can buy your food and a drink for $4, which is within your budget. But, you also know that you can't buy your food and two drinks because you don't have enough money in your budget.

A budget is a way to keep track of your income and expenses (spending). For example, if your monthly expenses are $1,100 and your income is $1,000 you will have to make adjustments so that you are not spending more than what you are making.

On your wish list you have a computer. You choose to start saving $100 a month to buy your computer. By keeping track of your expenses you know where you can make adjustments to save $200. $100 to stay within your income and $100 to save for your computer.

A budget helps you to make sure you don't spend more money than you have. What a disaster it could be if you didn't have a budget written down somewhere.

Budgets can also help you set aside money to save, pay bills, and to plan ahead for things that you don't pay for every month (such as auto insurance, tuition, computer, etc).

In my experience it is helpful to write out a budget. Just like a map for your money it will help you get to where you want to be. Without it you will be guessing about how you are going to get there.

Review your budget every month and make adjustments as needed. Make it into a game and see how much you can save in one month, then see if you can save a little more the second month, then a little more the third month.

FIVE

5.0 WHERE TO STASH YOUR CASH

When we talk about money most people think about cash like dollar bills and coins. Having cash is good, but it's better to keep your cash in a bank or credit union instead of in a pillow under your bed.

Pillow of cash at home

- Cash can be stolen
- Cash can catch on fire and too bad, so sad
- Dog can eat your cash and that's going to be messy

Cash at a Bank or Credit Union

- You can easily get your money
- Cannot be stolen from a bank
- Keeps it in one place
- Pay with debit cards instead of cash
- Single place to track all your cash

5.1 BANK OR CREDIT UNION

I am sure you have decided that you'll keep your money in a bank or credit union instead of your pillow under the bed.

Most people use a bank instead of a credit union. One of the main reasons is that anyone can open an account at a bank, but you have to qualify to be a member of a credit union, so it's probably easier for you to open your first account at a bank.

Ask your parents and friends where they bank and if it's close to where you live, then it's probably a good idea to try that bank first. You can always change your mind later, take your money out and move it to another bank.

Later on you may want to open an account at a credit union. They usually offer better rates and charge less fees than banks. I believe you should save money in as many ways as possible.

Bank and Credit Union Comparison

Bank

- Many locations (Bank of America has over 6100 locations)
- ATMs for big banks are probably close to you
- Charge higher fees and pay lower interest on savings
- Banks offer checking and savings accounts
- All banks insure money up to $100,000
- Anyone can open a bank account

Credit Union

- Fewer locations (Navy Credit Union has over 225 locations)
- ATMs for your credit union are not likely to be everywhere
- Charge lower fees and pay higher interest on savings
- Credit Unions offer share draft account (which are checking/savings accounts)
- Most Credit Unions are insured up to $100,000
- You have to qualify to be a member to open an account

5.2 TYPES OF ACCOUNTS

Savings Accounts are used to save money. You should consider having two savings accounts. One for short-term goals, which are items to be purchased in less than a year (like computer, tires, prom, vacation), and the other is for emergencies.

Checking Accounts are used for everyday purchases and to pay bills using Internet banking and checks.

Many banks and credit unions offer student savings and checking accounts. I recommend you ask the banker what choices they offer for students and how it compares to the regular savings and checking accounts. If you are under 18, you will need to bring a parent or guardian with you to open an account.

Six

6.0 So, you want to play cards?

Any game that uses cards has winners and losers. I want you to be a winner at the card game when it comes to your money. There are two cards in the banking game.

Banks will give you a debit card when you open up a checking account or mail it later to your home. They may also offer to give you a credit card as well.

Debit Card

You will be given a debit card when you open your checking account. When you use your debit card to buy something, the money spent comes out of your checking account.

You will have to create a 4-digit PIN (Personal Identification Number) when you get your debit card. Do not use your birthday for your PIN in case your card is stolen (thieves can look up your birthday). Don't use the last four digits on the card either; if your card is stolen the thieves will try to get into your account with the last four digits of your card.

A debit card is an easy and safe way to access your money. You can buy things or get cash out of the bank using an ATM (Automated Teller Machine).

A debit card is a benefit to you and a good card for you to have.

Credit Card

The bank will most likely try to give you a Credit Card. These types of cards don't take money out of your checking account, but add to a loan account anytime you use the credit card to buy something.

Banks make their money from the interest you pay on loans, so they probably will try to convince you that you need one. Tell the banker, "Thank you, but I'm not interested in one right now." (Yes, throw the word "interest" right back at them!)

Even if you say you're not interested, banks are serious about making money. So, it's likely they will continue to encourage you to get a credit card and they are trained to say things like:

Banker Says	Banker Means
It doesn't cost you anything	We'll make $ when you use it
It's free	We'll make $ when you use it
No interest if you pay off the balance	We know most don't, so we can make $
Good for emergencies	Good for emergency *want* buying so we can make $

6.1 CREDIT CARDS SUCK

- Credit Companies make it appealing for you to get a credit card. They will start with a 0% to 1.99% introductory rate which can very quickly jump to 14% to 19% if the amount owed is not paid off.

- Making the minimum payment will be costly, by making the minimum payment you will be paying more interest.

- If you charged $2,000.00 and made the minimum payment you would pay $1,077,00 in interest.

- If you make the minimum payment the purchase could end up costing you twice to three times the amount you spent.

- If you make a late payment the bank can increase the interest rate up to 29% from the U.S Average of 15%.

- The average household credit card debt is $14,500.

- Credit card debt in the US is over $8,000,000,000,000.

- Credit card companies make almost $60,000,000,000 a year.

- Credit cards don't help people. They make credit card companies rich and you don't want to be part of this mess. Trust me on this one.

6.2 AN INTERESTING PICTURE WORTH A THOUSAND WORDS

Here's a picture that shows you what credit cards cost for the average household.

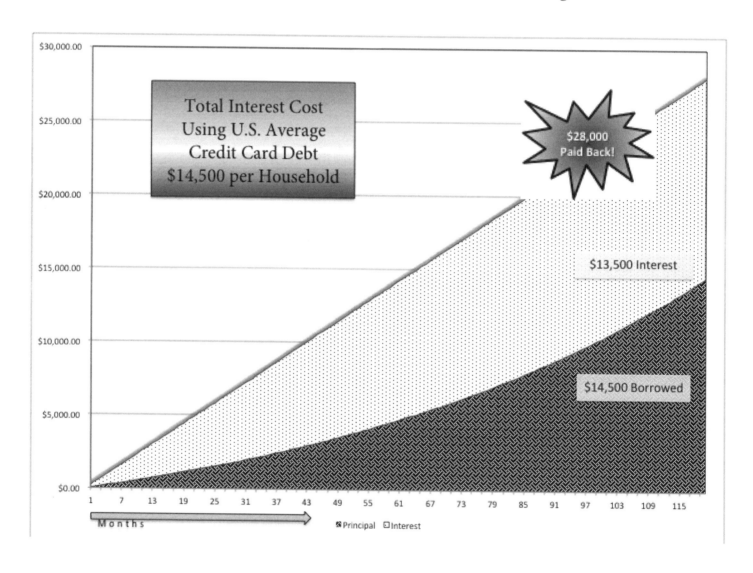

6.3 HOW TO AVOID AN EXPENSIVE LESSON

By keeping track of all your day-to-day spending, you can make sure that you never spend more money than you have in your checking account (overdraw). This often happens because you lost track of your money in the bank.

Overdrawing your account can be expensive as the overdraft fee can be $10 or more. I know a girl who learned this lesson the hard way. She didn't keep track of her account balance and was overdrawn. Over the weekend, she went to McDonalds for a $1 ice cream cone and to 7/11 to buy gum for a $1. Of course she stopped a few more places over the weekend.

Ice Cream Cone	$1 + $10 Overdraft Fee = $11
Pack of Gum	$1 + $10 Overdraft Fee = $11
Value Tea	$1 + $10 Overdraft Fee = $11
Lotion	$3 + $10 Overdraft Fee = $13
Parking	$2 + $10 Overdraft Fee = $12
Ear buds (sale)	$9 + $10 Overdraft Fee = $19
TJ Maxx	$11 + $10 Overdraft Fee = $21

She spent $28.00 and paid $70.00 in overdraft fees.

She had to pay the bank for teaching her the lesson of always knowing her bank account balance. Learning from her experience can save you money. Keep track of your money to avoid this expensive lesson.

You can check your account balance online. You can set up a balance alerts, the bank will send you a text with your account balance.

Seven

7.0 are your workers lazy?

Do you know Mr. Bill? You may know him better by his first name, "Dollar." Sometimes Bill can be lazy and do no work. Then again, Bill can be the best worker in the world. The harder Bill works, the more money you make. When Bill is lazy and doesn't work, you don't make any money.

You are Bill's boss and if you don't make him work hard, then he will do little or nothing, year after year. Remember, the harder Bill works, the more money you make.

If you let 10,000 Bills sit in a pillow under your bed doing nothing, then after a year you have 10,000 Bills still doing nothing. After 10 more years you still have 10,000 Bills doing nothing. How much did Bill's laziness cost you using the Rule of 72?

Remember, how I explained that you could win the Lotto without playing? It was by making Bill work hard for you. The harder Bill worked (higher annual return) the faster you made more money. The longer the time you let your money work for you, the greater the difference because of compounding interest and our friend, the Rule of 72. Don't ever let your Bills be lazy workers. You are paying for their laziness with your future earnings.

7.1 Investing

Investing is buying something that makes Bill work hard for you. There are three common investment types.

- Real Estate
- Stock Market
- Business

7.2 Real Estate

We'll start with real estate because it is easy to understand. Real estate is a fancy word for any building and land, like a house.

I find it fascinating that Ray Kroc who made McDonald's into a 100 billion dollar restaurant company said, "We are in the real estate business, not the hamburger business." McDonalds makes most of their money by owning the restaurant's real estate and charging the franchise owners rent, not from selling their McMeals.

You make money when you buy real estate and charge rent to someone who needs to use your property to live at or for work. If the rent is higher than the cost of the loan payment and maintenance, then you make money.

I don't want to get into all the details of real estate investment calculations, but I want you to be aware that it's not only about the rent money. The value of real estate growth over time is significant.

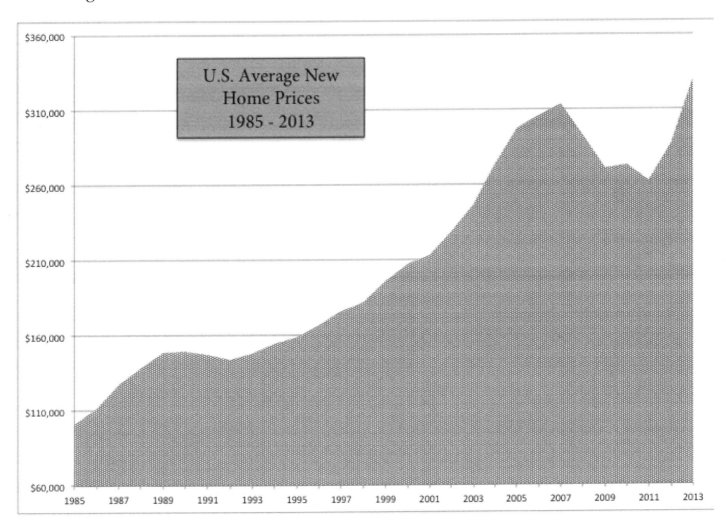

U.S. Average New
Home Prices
1985 - 2013

7.3 STOCK MARKET

The stock market began around 400 years ago when English merchants didn't have enough money to start huge factories. To raise money, the merchants would meet at a coffee house to buy and sell small partnerships of their businesses in pieces called "shares." Over time, the trading of shares became very big and they changed the name of the coffee house to the stock market.

You make money in the stock market when the stock you own increases in price. You can also lose money when the stock you own decreases in price.

Almost every major company you can think of is traded in the stock market and you can buy and sell stocks in these companies. Want to own a share of Disney, Apple, Wal-Mart, Coca Cola, McDonalds, Verizon, AT&T, Chevron, and Target? No problem, it's easy to open a brokerage account (you have to be over 18) at Fidelity, E*Trade, Scottrade, or any other stock trading business.

I listed some popular companies off the top of my head, but I thought you might be interested to see how the prices went up and down over 18 years for a few of the companies I mentioned:

Company	1995	2000	2005	2010	2013	Gain
Disney	$15	$31	$29	$33	$65	333%
Apple	$10	$32	$44	$260	$442	4,320%
Wal-Mart	$13	$52	$50	$54	$76	484%
Coca Cola	$13	$29	$22	$27	$42	223%
McDonald's	$18	$34	$30	$69	$100	400%

The stock market fluctuates up and down every day, every year, and has gone up in overall value since it began. Below is a graph of the Dow Jones Industrial Index (DJIA), which is a good indicator of the stock market. It contains an average of 30 companies that reflect the overall health of the stock market. Companies on the DJIA include McDonalds, Home Depot, Coca Cola, AT&T, Disney, etc. If you bought stock of every company in the DJIA, you would have the same result that you see on the graph below.

Take a look at the value of the stock index in 2000 and compare it to the far right hand value in 2013. The value was $4,000 and now it's over $15,000. So your money would have gone up in value by 282% if you had bought shares of the companies in the DJIA in 2000.

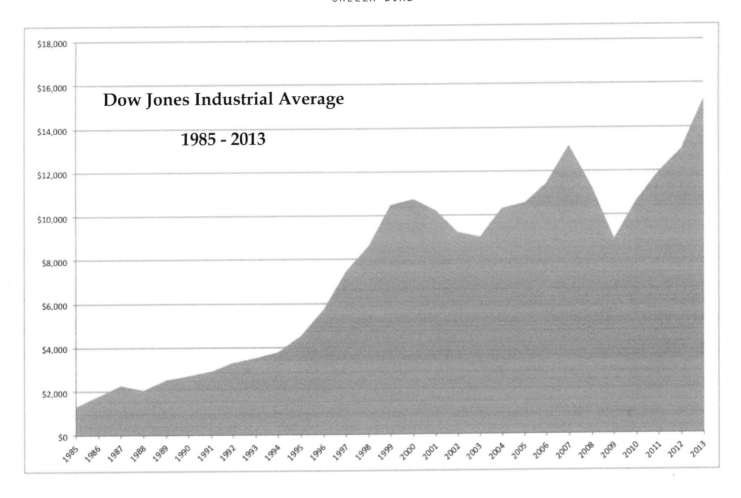

7.4 BUSINESS

Owning a business sounds like fun, but this book is about making money not having fun. Owning a small business has the highest risk of the three types of investment. It is the most dangerous investment because the failure rate of a small business in the second year is 25% and the chance of a business surviving five years is 50%. These are conservative estimates. If you Google "small business failure" you will find failure rates as high as 90% in the first year, particularly in the restaurant industry.

Owning a business can lead to great personal satisfaction and make you wealthy. Many people have done it, every large company you know was started by someone.

My advice for most of you is to hold off on starting your own business until you have the other two types of investments generating more money than you could lose in a year by starting your own business. That way you are covered in case your business fails and you've only lost one year of investment income. If you don't wait, then it could seriously damage your financial dreams for many years to come.

EIGHT

8.0 DIVERSIFY

Just saying the word "diversify" makes you sound money smart. If you are learning and paying attention, you are already money smart, but there's more to learn on your journey to becoming rich. You also need to know how to stay rich and not lose your wealth.

There is a point in time when you need to diversify your money and not keep it in a single investment. <u>Diversification</u> means that you spread your money over multiple types of investments. Don't keep all your money only in the stock market, real estate or business. Diversification of your investments will help to balance out risk. If all of your money was in the stock market and it crashed by 90%, you would be left with only 10%. It's the same with real estate (houses and buildings) and businesses.

It's just like eggs, so let's think of money as eggs. If you kept all of your eggs in one basket and accidentally dropped the basket, you could lose all your eggs. If you split up your eggs into several baskets, one for real estate, one for stocks and one for business, then dropping a single basket would not be a big loss.

Nine

9.0 Hope is not a plan

Some people will *hope* to become rich, but I want you to *plan* to become rich. You could lie in bed and hope to become a doctor for your whole life, but the fact is that if you want to become a doctor then you are going to have to make a plan to get there. The same applies to your money. Hope is not a plan. Plan now because time is on your side and you cannot make time up. Every year counts, every dollar counts, every investment counts towards your plan.

9.1 Your plan to wealth

You need to remember these key points towards your future plans. Read them until you can repeat them from memory.

- Knowledge about money will make me wealthy and will change my life for the better
- I think about *need* or *want* before buying something. I control my *wants*.
- I remember the power of Rule 72 compound interest.
- I invest my money as soon as I can.
- I stay away from credit cards.
- I borrow money like the rich, not like the poor.
- Every dollar should be working as hard as possible to make me rich.
- I diversify to protect myself against one bad investment.
- I think repeatedly about my plans to get to my first million and how it will change my life.

9.2 THE END OF THIS BOOK IS THE BEGINNING OF YOUR MONEY JOURNEY

Being wealthy means more than just having money, you have to be wealthy in your heart and help others. I believe it's true that by helping others, we help ourselves. Have a good heart and help others.

Right now, you can help your friends and family by sharing what you have learned. It can be a life changing experience for someone. What if you never shared your knowledge of money with them?

I am confident that you can make a plan, follow it, and reach your goals to become wealthy. Now you have the money knowledge and the time to make your dreams a reality. Nothing will bring me more joy than for you to begin your money journey towards wealth and happiness now.

CD

You can find additional resources on my website: www.moneybasics101.com

You can also email your questions to: teens@moneybasics101.com

Appendix

Sample Spending Plan

Places to shop and save money

How to open checking and savings accounts

List of credit unions

How to write a check

SAMPLE SPENDING PLAN

Expense Type	Income	Cost	Available $ $ $
Home			-
Rent			-
Telephone			-
Furniture/appliances			-
School Supplies			-
Books			-
Supplies			-
Food			-
Groceries			-
Snacks			-
Transportation			-
Car payment			-
Insurance			-
Car registration			-
Gas			-
Repairs/Maintenance			-
Clothing			-
Clothes, shoes			-
Entertainment			-
Going Out			-
Movies			-
Concerts			-
Clubs			-
Miscellaneous			-
Birthday Party			-
Parents gifts			-

Places to shop and save money

- .99 Cent store

- Amazon.com

- Church Sales

- Craig's List (My friend bought all the furniture in her house from Craig's List)

- Dollar Tree

- Garage sales in your neighborhood or surrounding areas

- JC Penney sales

- Kohl's

- Ross

- Savers

- Sears sales

- Target

- Thrift Shops (You can find them in all different cities.)

- TJ Maxx

- Used Appliance, battery, book, electronic, furniture, tire stores etc.

HOW TO OPEN CHECKING AND SAVINGS ACCOUNTS

How to open a checking account in 4 easy steps :

1. Bring at least $100 to open your Checking Account and <u>two </u>forms of identification (one with a picture like: student ID, Library card, Social Security card, Birth certificate, Immunization record).

2. Go to the bank and tell someone in new accounts that you want to open a Checking Account.

3. They will help you fill out the checking application and will ask you for ID and the money to open the account.

4. You will get temporary checks, a debit card, and a big smile from the banker.

How to open a Savings Account in 4 easy steps:

1. Bring at least $25 to open your Saving Account two forms of identification (one with a picture like: student ID, Library card, Social Security card, Birth certificate, Immunization record).

2. Go to the bank and tell someone in new accounts that you want to open a Savings Account.

3. They will help you fill out the savings application and will ask you for your ID and the money to open the account.

4. You will get a statement of your deposit and a big smile from the banker.

LIST OF CREDIT UNIONS

You can find a listing of Credit Unions near you at:

http://credituniondirectory.net/

How to write a check

ASHLEY RICHGIRL
101 ELM ST.
SEASIDE, TX 80777

16-49 7002
1220

0011

DATE _____

PAY TO THE
ORDER OF _____ $ _____

_____ DOLLARS

ABCBANK
ABCBANK.COM

FOR _____ _____

A123000567 1122004901B 0011

ASHLEY RICHGIRL
101 ELM ST.
SEASIDE, TX 80777

16-49 7002
1220

0012

DATE _____7/4/2014_____

PAY TO THE
ORDER OF ___The United Way Charity_____ $ _2,051.00_

___Two Thousand Fifty One and 00/100___ DOLLARS

ABCBANK
ABCBANK.COM

FOR _Donation_____ _____Ashley Richgirl_____

A123000567 1122004901B 0012

Notes

Notes

Notes